British Firearms

The Lee Enfield Number 1 Rifles

By Alan M. Petrillo

Published by Excalibur Publications

By the same author from Excalibur Publications:
British Service Rifles & Carbines 1888-1900
Cartridge Carbines of the British Army
The Lee Enfield Number 4 Rifles
The Number 5 Jungle Carbine

Excalibur Publications
PO Box 89667, Tucson, AZ 85752-9667
(520) 575-9057
excalibureditor@earthlink.net

ISBN-10: 1-880677-01-6
ISBN-13: 978-1-880677-01-8
6P311

Table of Contents

Dedication

For Gayle, the best friend a husband ever had.

Introduction

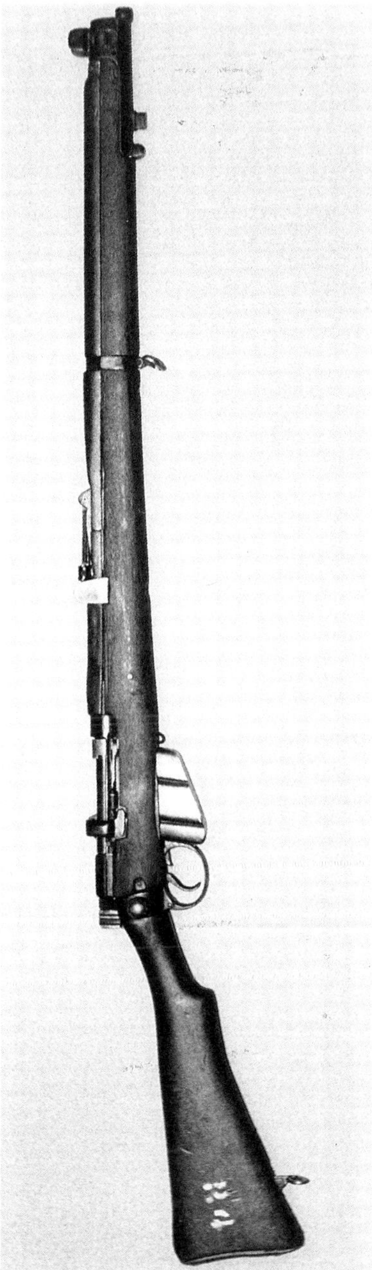

The Number 1 series rifles took the British soldier from the turn of the century into the Second World War.

The SMLE, or "Smelly," as it was affectionately called by British troops, was a true product of the turn of the twentieth century. Born early in the 1900s, the rifle was a radical departure from military thinking of the time, for it was designed as a rifle for all troops — infantry, artillery and cavalry. This was a change from previous military procedure of a long rifle for the infantry, and a carbine for the artillery and cavalry.

And even more astonishing, is the fact that the rifle was developed by the British military bureaucracy, a thoroughly conservative group of individuals which was used to taking its time in the development of arms, and especially when it came to radical change.

But change the British did, and they earned the praise and accolades of their troopers about the new rifle. As might be expected, there was the usual grousing and complaints about the SMLE when it was first introduced, but these were quickly dealt with and the rifle modified to rectify minor problems.

Thus, the SMLE, later called the Number 1 rifle, was to continue in production through the early years of the Second World War.

This, then, is about the rifle that carried the British troopers through the heart of the twentieth century — through the Great War, and well on into World War II.

General History

While investigations into a shortened rifle were conducted prior to the second Boer War of 1899-1900, it was not until late in the first year of the new century that British authorities were truly confronted with an opportunity to make a change from the longer barreled Lee Enfield then in service with British troops.

Late in 1900, the Superintendent of the Royal Small Arms Factory at Enfield (RSAF) petitioned the Small Arms Committee, which had charge of developing a new rifle, to consider adoption of a shorter rifle based heavily on the then-current arm. The Superintendent pointed out that the current rifle had proven itself as reliable, and that certain modifications would make the arm even better, but in a different form.

The Superintendent was aware of the fact that to re-equip the Army with all new rifles would cost a staggering sum, especially if new tooling was required. Accordingly, he suggested using existing tooling to produce a new short rifle, based on the predecessor Lee Enfield.

His suggestions included a maximum weight for the rifle of 8 pounds 6 ounces, improved sighting, and provisions for loading by charger. These changes, the Superintendent maintained, would not only produce a fine service arm, but could be done for approximately the same cost as that of the then-current service rifle.

Modifications suggested to the service arm by the Superintendent of RSAF

Number 1 Rifle Statistics

Model	Adoption Date	Changes in Pattern
No.1MkI	23 December 1902	Shortened rifle Completely new pattern New sights, barrel
No.1MkI*	2 July 1906	Gunmetal buttplate Improved magazine New butt swivel
No.1MkI**	4 January 1908	Sighting modifications
No.1MkI***	22 April 1914	New foresight New rearsight
No.1MkI Cond.	2 November 1903	Sample patterns only
No.1MkII Cond.	16 January 1903	New safety catch SMLE magazine
No.1MkII* Cond.	2 July 1906	Sheet steel buttplate
No.1MkII** Cond.	25 June 1908	Conversion for Navy
No.1MkIII	26 January 1907	Improved sights Fixed charger bridge
No.1MkIII*	2 January 1916	Omitted volley sights Cocking piece modified No rearsight windgauge
No.1MkV	1922	Aperture rearsight No volley sights One-piece handguard
No.1MkVI	1926	Flat-sided receiver Heavier barrel Improved rearsight

Enfield included:

- Charger loading for the rifle
- A new type of charger, to hold five cartridges
- A shorter and lighter barrel
- A new method of fixing the front sight
- A special nosecap on the forend to which the bayonet would be fixed
- Removal of the safety catch
- A new design of rearsight with a sliding leaf
- A double pull-off on the trigger to allow for more consistent shooting
- Longer handguards

Various service rifles were modified to these specifications and put through rigorous testing at the School of Musketry, located at Hythe, as well as among other smaller units around the country. These tests resulted in a number of changes being made to the pattern of the rifles, notably in the depth of the rifling in the barrel, to the sights, and the magazine.

It was found that the normal Enfield rifling did not give sufficient velocity for the new arm, so the rifling was modified so that it was

The Number 1 Mark III rifle was the workhorse of the First World War, and earned the reputation as the fastest military turnbolt rifle in the world.

deeper at the muzzle. This solved the velocity problem.

The rearsight went through several patterns, each showing a modification in the ramp, slide and gradations in order to arrive at the proper pattern.

The magazine difficulties were those which went back to the Boer War when sand and dirt clogged magazine springs. The pattern of magazine at the time did not allow for removal of the follower and spring, thus complicating cleaning by

Magazine Differences

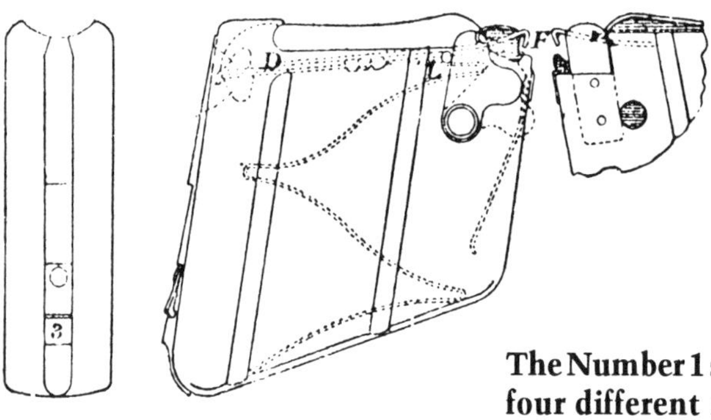

Magazine No.3

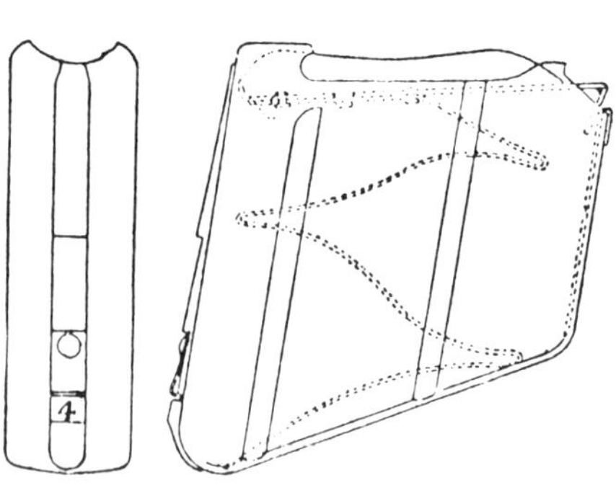

Magazine No. 4

The Number 1 series rifles used four different magazines during its lifetime. The first version made its appearance with the Number 1 Mark I, followed by magazine No.2 for the Mark 1*. This magazine had a straight end and a deeper case to assist in loading. These two models were used with the Mark VI ammunition. The No.3 and No.4 magazines were used with later rifles for the Mark VII ammunition, which featured a pointed bullet instead of a round nose.

the troops. The modified magazine for the new rifle had an easily removed spring and follower.

Ultimately, 1,000 rifles were manufactured for trial by approximately 20 units of the Royal Marines, Royal Navy, Cavalry and Infantry. The Small Arms Committee had to deal with a considerable amount of criticism regarding the design of the new rifle. The shorter barrel caused the greatest amount of consternation, especially among the target shooting elite of Bisley. It was charged that the lighter, shorter barrel could not possibly improve the accuracy over the older Lee Enfield, but rather deteriorate it. Another criticism was that the lightness of the rifle would also cause greater recoil, also adversely affecting accuracy. But while the criticism continued, the Small Arms Committee began the trial.

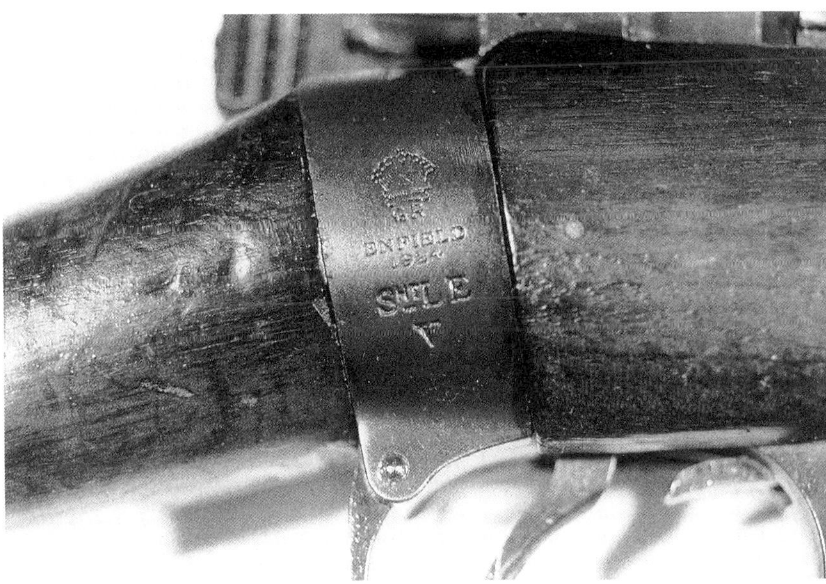

Markings on Number 1 rifles were generally on the right side of the butt socket. Here could be found the crown and cypher, the name of the arsenal which made the weapon, the date manufactured, and the model designation. In this instance, this is a Number 1 Mark V made at Enfield in 1924.

The distinctive nosecap of the Number 1 rifles make them readily identifiable from their contemporaries. This nosecap is on a Number 1 Mark I rifle and features the inward-curving ears found on those early rifles.

The trial featured the then-current service rifle, the Lee Enfield (now commonly called a Long Lee Enfield) and the new shortened rifle. The rifles were to be fired one after the other in each part of the trial in order to be sure that they were compared under similar conditions. The trial consisted of testing the rifles as follows:

• Each rifle was to fire seven shots deliberate fire, from any position, at 200, 500 and 800 yards. This was to be done twice.

• Moving targets were to be fired twice, seven shots per rifle each time.

• Vanishing targets were to be fired twice, seven shots per rifle each time.

• Snap shooting was also to be fired twice, seven shots per rifle each time.

• Rapid fire was to be shot at 200 yards for one and a half minutes, and at 600 yards for three minutes. The 600 yard stage was repeated with the shortened rifle charged with a full magazine, and then recharged with 10 cartridges.

• Long range fire was to be shot at 2,000 yards against horizontal canvas screens at least 50 yards square. This was done once, firing 15 rounds per rifle.

• With bayonets fixed, the shortened rifles were fired 30 rounds rapid fire at 200 yards.

• In order to compare the different foresights on the two rifles, they were fired at varying ranges at large and small objects colored to blend into the background. This was shot in various light to simulate widely divergent conditions.

Eventually, the reports from the various units testing the rifles were accumulated by the Small Arms Committee and the overwhelming opinion was that the shortened rifle should be adopted.

The new type of charger loading was much favored by those testing the shortened rifles, and was found to be very quick and easy to handle. The new sights also found many positive recommendations, especially the windgauge on the rearsight.

After review and more testing, the Small Arms Committee agreed to more modifications, including:

• A barleycorn foresight
• A foresight protector with the top of the hood removed
• An adjusting screw on the rearsight elevation slide
• Tighter chargers and charger guides
• A deeper magazine case
• Milling a slot in the body for a cutoff
• A new form of stocking up.

From all this work and effort, the Rifle, Short, Magazine, Lee Enfield, Mark I was officially born on 23 December, 1902.

When discussing the SMLE series of rifles, it is important to remember that the British changed the nomenclature of the series, along with all their other series of rifles, in May of 1926. All the SMLE series rifles became known as the

The Change in Rearsights

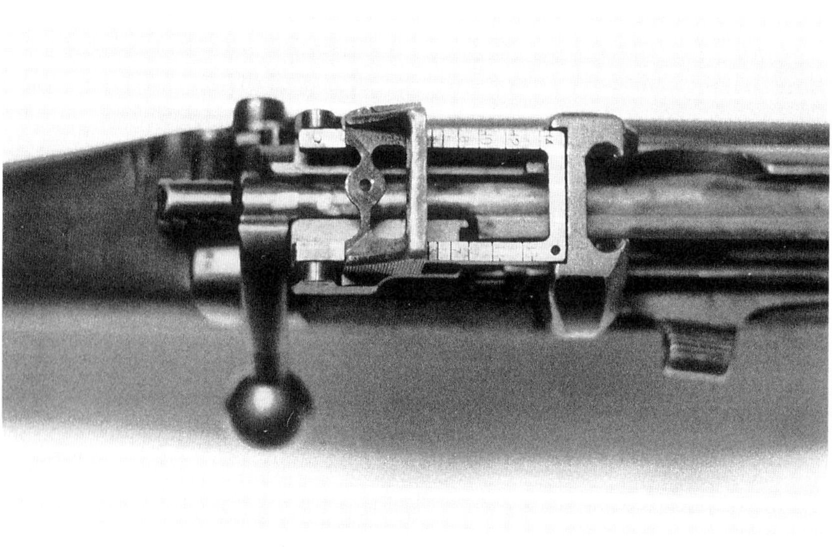

The Number 1 Mark I rearsight, top, was a radical departure from its predecessor on the Lee Enfield rifle, being adjustable for windage as well as elevation. The Mark V rearsight, bottom, was the first Lee Enfield rearsight to be mounted on the receiver instead of the barrel.

Mark I to Mark V

Both the Number 1 Mark I (top) and Mark V (bottom) rearsights are shown in raised positions. Note the similar silhouette on the Mark V to the later Number 4 Mark 1 rifle.

Number 1 series. For example, the SMLE Mark I became the Rifle No. 1 Mark I, while the SMLE Mark III changed to the Rifle No. 1 Mark III.

Other series were the Number 2 (.22LR training rifles), Number 3 (the Pattern 14 rifle and its brothers), the Number 4 (World War II and Korea-era rifles) and the Number 5 (the jungle carbine).

Number 1 Mark I

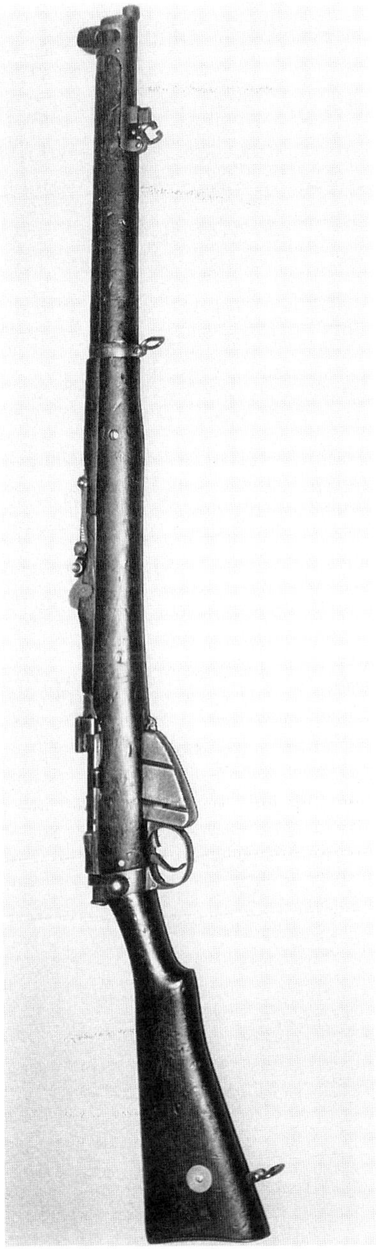

The Number 1 Mark I rifle was officially adopted in 1902.

Rifle, Short, Magazine, Lee Enfield, Mark I (Number 1 Mark I)

Commonly known as the SMLE, for Short, Magazine, Lee Enfield, this rifle was to lead a parade of weapons which would serve the British Commonwealth though two world wars. It was designed around the idea that it would be a "shorter" rifle for the infantryman, and a "longer" carbine for everyone else — cavalrymen, artillerymen, engineers, and others.

The rifle, approved on 23 December 1902, was a full-stocked weapon, without any part of the barrel protruding from the forestock, except for the very tip of the muzzle. Thus, the Number 1 series of Lee Enfields is readily identifiable, since the wood furniture runs out to the end of the weapon.

The Number 1 series of rifles came into being because of the many difficulties experienced by British troops at the hand of the Boers in the South African War at the turn of the century. Three of the major improvements sought by the upper echelons of British commanders were more efficient loading by use of a charger, less weight, and improved sighting. The then-current issue Lee Enfield Mark 1* rifle, commonly called the Long Lee Enfield, was not fitted with a charging mechanism to allow reloading of the magazine by charger.

In the end, the final result of the SMLE's development led to the adoption of a rifle with a receiver remarkably similar to its predecessor. It was a round action rifle, with provision for a detachable magazine of 10 rounds. However, the new action incorporated a safety into the left rear side, as opposed to the previous rifle's safety at the rear of the cocking piece. This new safety incorporated a lever and catch, which were fixed to the receiver by a washer, spring and screw. When the safety was operated, the catch engaged a recess in

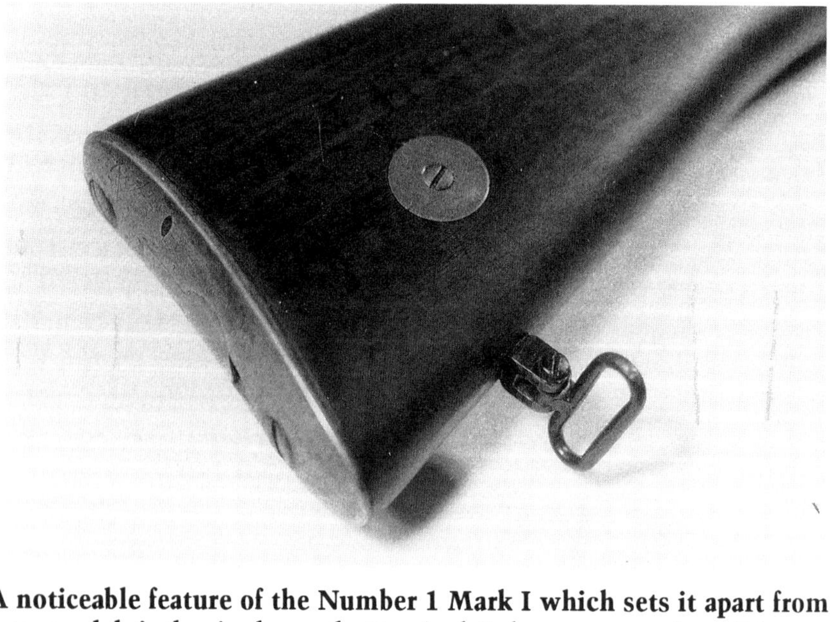

A noticeable feature of the Number 1 Mark I which sets it apart from later models is the single post butt swivel. Subsequent versions did away with the post.

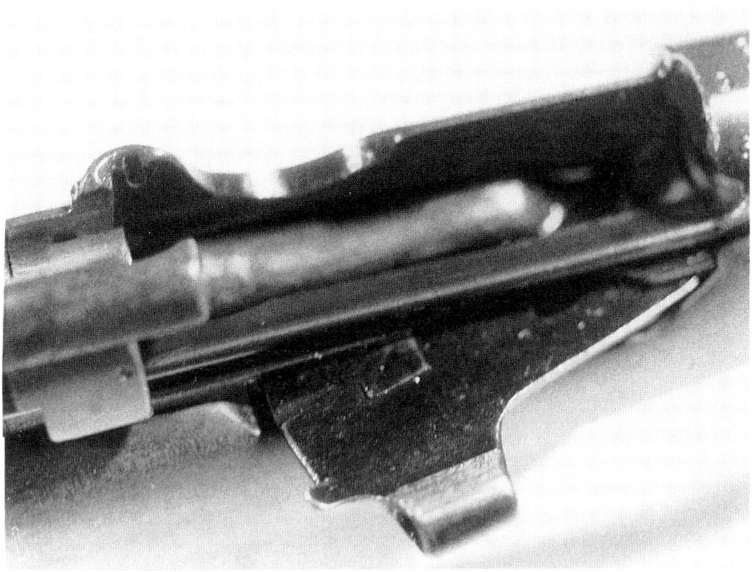

The magazine cutoff continued to be used on the Number 1 series rifles. This sheet steel plate allowed the soldier to use the rifle as a single loader, while keeping a full magazine below it in reserve.

the cocking piece to prohibit movement of the bolt.

The trigger of the Number 1 Mark I was again pinned to the trigger guard, as was its predecessor, but the upper part of the trigger was very different. Instead of the circular recess of the previous trigger, the new model featured two ribs or nubs which bore on the lower arm of the sear. The effect of the two nubs was to produce a double pull-off of 3 to 4 pounds for the first pull, and 5 to 6 pounds for the second. The first pull is the "slack" known to anyone who has ever fired a military rifle.

With the change in triggers, it also was necessary to make a change in the rifle's sear. This required lengthening and otherwise altering the shape of the lower arm of the sear in order to properly engage the new trigger.

The Number 1 Mark I bolt was very similar to earlier rifles, differing chiefly in the length of the striker, the cocking piece, and in minor modifications to the bolthead.

The bolt body was the standard Lee Enfield type with a long locking shoulder at the top right, with a smaller locking lug about halfway down the bolt body and on the opposite side of the long lug. The smaller lug engaged a recess in the left of the receiver body, while the long locking shoulder engaged the right rear of the upper receiver.

The cocking piece was of shorter dimensions than that on the earlier Lee Enfield rifles, since the pro-

Mark I Rearsight

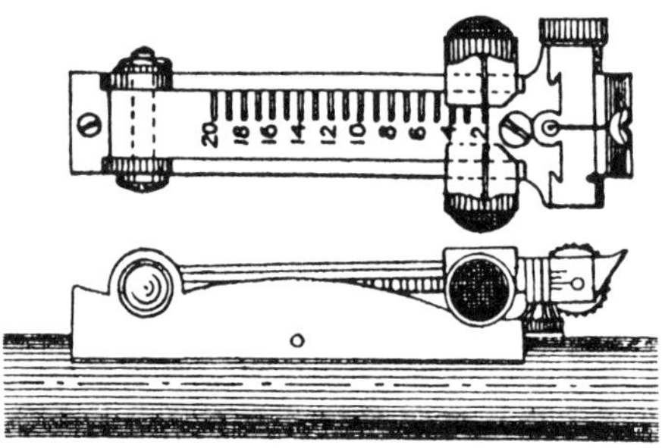

Two views of the rearsight on the Number 1 Mark I rifle. At left, the illustration shows two elevations of the sight, while the photo at the bottom depicts the rearsight in conjunction with the rearsight protection ears, attached to the snap-on rear handguard.

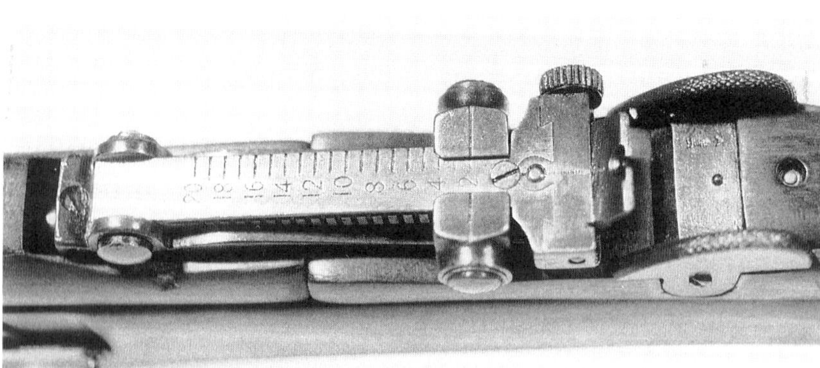

jections for a safety catch had been discontinued. It also was milled to receive two recesses for the safety catch attached to the left of the receiver.

The bolthead was similar to the previous type found on earlier rifles, but was modified in a major way. In order to provide for charger loading through use of a .303 British clip, a guide was mounted on the left side of the receiver and a sliding charger guide to mate with it was attached to the rifle's bolthead.

To use the charging arrangement, the bolt was pulled to the rear until the back of the charger guide on the bolthead struck a projection on the receiver and was pushed forward to align with the guide on the receiver. At that point, the infantryman could insert a charger and strip the rounds into the magazine. While this arrangement was certainly serviceable, troopers ultimately found that the sliding fixture was less than robust, and sometimes broke at the most inopportune moment.

The rearsight on the Number 1 Mark I rifle was a departure from previous rifles, being a sliding leaf type protected by heavy wings. The "V" notch battle sight was zeroed for firing at 300 yards with the bayonet fixed. In addition, provision was made on the leaf for settings to 2,000 yards, with adjustments being made by bone knobs on the sides of the slide.

New to this series of rifles was the provision of a windgauge on the rearsight, allowing the infantryman the opportunity to adjust the rearsight for deflection. This was accomplished through a small adjusting wheel at the right of the sight.

British practice at the time called for sections and platoons to use volley firing at ranges beyond 1,500 yards. Accordingly, the new pattern SMLE was fitted with dial sights on the left side of the rifle. The sights consisted of a dial plate and aiming pointer inletted into the left center of the forend and held in place by a screw which passed through the forend. The dial plate was graduated from 1,600 to 2,800 yards.

The rear part of the dial sights was a folding aperture affixed at the safety lever. In practice, the trooper would set the aiming pointer on the dial plate to the intended range, raise the rear aperture, sight along the axis of the aperture and pointer, and then fire on command.

Pin-point accuracy was not the hallmark of the long range dial sights. Instead, the British used volley firing as interdiction or harassing fire.

Essentially, a section of infantrymen would be placed in firing order and be given a specific yardage figure at which they would set their dial sights. Having done this, and on command of their officer or sergeant, the section would fire a volley at some distant target.

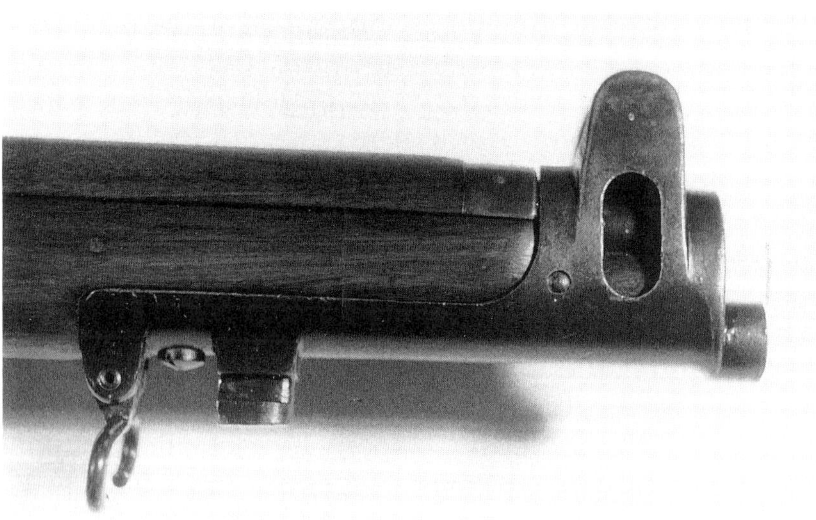

The foresight of the Number 1 Mark I was protected by a large, heavy nosecap, with inward-curving ears. The nosecap contained a boss and stud for mounting a blade bayonet, and also had a provision for a stacking swivel.

A unique charging system was fitted to the Number 1 Mark I rifle in the form of a bolthead charging sytem. A sliding charger guide was affixed to the bolthead of the rifle, which, when the breech bolt was withdrawn to the rear, mated with a recess in the left of the body. This allowed a charger filled with five cartridges to be placed between the two, and for the cartridges to be pressed into the magazine.

This whole process was quite involved and took place amid a great deal of order-shouting and foot-stomping on the part of the officer or sergeant. The number of rounds fired would depend on the nature of the target, and the intent of the commanders in keeping the enemy busy.

The effect on the receiving end of volley fire was a rain of lead. Perhaps the fire was not accurately placed in terms of modern-day sniping, but it covered a specific section of ground with harassing fire. At the time, the psychological effect of having an enemy interdict your freedom of movement with relatively direct fire from more than 2,000 yards away was staggering.

The foresight on the Number 1 Mark 1 rifle was a barleycorn type affixed in a dovetail slot on a sheet metal base pinned to the rifle's barrel. The barleycorn was made in three sizes — normal, high and low — and differed by .015 inch each.

The foresight could be shifted in the dovetail slot to make changes in the bullet's point of impact.

The new rifle's barrel had external contours similar to those of its predecessor, but was strongly reinforced at the breech and was five inches shorter than the Long Lee Enfield's barrel.

The barrel was 25-3/16 inches long and featured the .303 inch Enfield five groove rifling of one turn in 10, left hand twist. The groove depth at the muzzle was .0065 inches, and .005 inches at the muzzle. The width of the lands was .0965 inches.

Front and rear handguards cover the barrel, and are secured by a band about midway along

Additional sighting was in the form of long range dial sights, often known as volley sights. These consisted of a dial plate inletted into the left side of the forend, to which was attached a pointer that served as the front aiming mark.

The rear part of the dial sight was a folding aperture, at left, which was affixed at the safety lever.

The purpose of using the dial sights was to harass the enemy with long range interdiction fire. Done properly, it had its intended effect.

the forend, and by a large steel nosecap. The band, often referred to as the middle or lower band, was hinged to accommodate the stock and made of blackened brass. The band was pieced to take a securing screw, which also carried the sling swivel.

The nosecap, which protects the foresight, was fashioned from steel stock and secured to the forend by front and rear nosecap screws. These engaged the nosecap horizontally and vertically, respectively. In addition to providing the large protecting wings for the foresight, the heavy nosecap featured a large boss and stud as securing points for the Pattern 1907 bayonet.

It should be noted that the ears which protect the foresight on the Number 1 Mark I are curved inwards, which serve as a distinct indicator when compared to later marks, such as the Mark III. A piling swivel also was fitted to the nosecap of the Mark I.

The front handguard covered the barrel from the nosecap to the rearsight base, and was retained in position by the lower band and the rear edge of the nosecap. This handguard incorporated two ears on its rear end which extend partially along the sides of the rearsight base.

The rear handguard is held in position on the barrel by a double jawed spring, and covers the barrel from the action body to the rearsight base. It incorporates two ears on its front end which also extend along the sides of the rearsight base. In addition, the rear handguard embodies a rearsight protector in the form of steel ears on each side.

The forend fitted around the underside of the body and barrel, and projected to within one-eighth inch from the muzzle. A stud and spring were fitted into a vertical recess in the forend, located under the nosecap. At the rear of the forend was a keeper plate, into which the squared end of the stock bolt fitted. This arrangement prevented the stock bolt from turning and loosening the butt stock.

The butt stock was made in three lengths — normal, short and long. The short and long versions each were one-half inch shorter or longer than the normal butt stock. They were stamped with an "S" or "L" respectively. The butt was fitted with a pedestal-type butt swivel and a steel butt plate, each secured by two screws. There was no trap in the butt plate.

On the lower right hand side of the butt stock, inletted into the wood, was a round brass disc, secured by a brass screw. This butt disc was used to receive stampings designating unit markings.

The magazine was a 10-round staggered column Lee box, which was slightly deeper than that on the previous rifle. It was made deeper because it was found that it was difficult to load the second five cartridges by charger. A zigzag spring was attached to the magazine platform, and was considered much stronger than its earlier counterparts.

A stop clip was provided on the magazine's right side in order to enable the assembly to be stripped for cleaning and to keep the right hand cartridge in the correct position.

The rifle's receiver featured a cutoff fitted into a slot cut in the right side. The function of the cutoff was to allow the trooper to keep the rifle's fully-charged magazine in reserve, and use the weapon as a single loader until such time as it was necessary to open the cutoff and use the rounds in the magazine.

Faced with a hard-charging enemy but yards away, the comfort of a full magazine of 10 rounds was not to be underestimated.

Number 1 Mark I*

Rifle, Short, Magazine, Lee Enfield, Mark I* (Number 1 Mark I*)

After the SMLE had passed into the hands of the British troops in the field, a number of deficiencies came to light and were dealt with by the Army. The corrections made to the rifle caused it to be designated the Mark I* model, the asterisk denoting that there had been modifications made from the Mark I pattern, which was sealed at the Enfield Pattern Room at Enfield Lock. The Mark I* rifle was officially approved 2 July 1906.

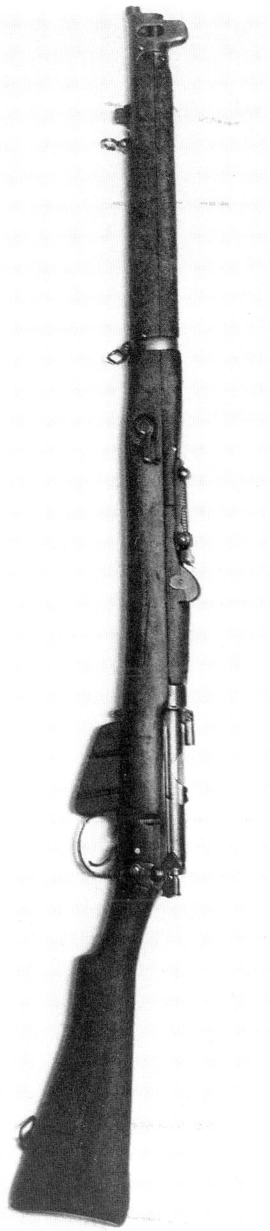

The Number 1 Mark I* corrected some deficiencies found in its predecessor.

One of the most noticeable changes in the rifle was that the buttplate was now made of gunmetal, and was fitted with a trap for cleaning gear and an oil bottle. The troops had complained that the previous mark rifle had too many sharp corners, so those were rounded as well.

In addition, a new type of

The action of the Number 1 Mark I* was the same as that of the Mark I rifle in profile, and indeed, in its fabrication. The bolt and charger guide, safety assembly, furniture, and long range sights all were carried on into this modification. Note the many date stampings to the right of the safety spring. This indicates the rifle has returned to the arsenal a number of times for subsequent repair work or modifications. In fact, this Mark I* carries the later type trigger guard with the sling swivel attachment at the front, instead of a link loop.

The nosecap of the Mark I* was the same version as that of its predecessor, with the noticable inward-curving protection ears. These ears were to be changed in later SMLE models. When compared with the later nosecaps, the curved ears of the Mark I and Mark I* look somewhat unusual.

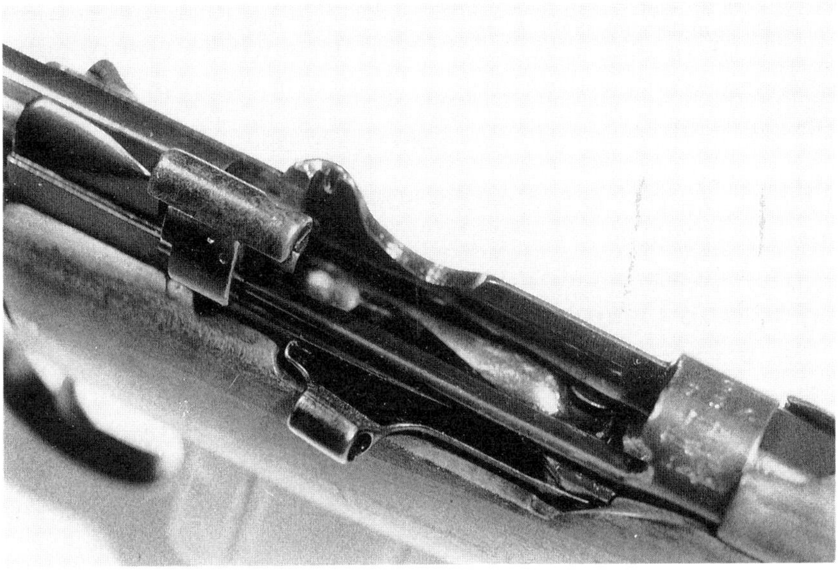

The magazine cutoff was fitted into a slot in the right side of the receiver, shown here in the closed position. To open the cutoff, the soldier grasped the knurled knob and pulled outward. The bolt on this rifle has been withdrawn to the rear so that the charger guide lines up with its mating recess in the left of the receiver.

The Safety Assembly

The safety assembly on the Number 1 series rifles is made up of four individual pieces—the safety lever, top, (callcd the locking bolt lever by the British); the safety catch itself, center, (threaded on the top of the lever; the safety screw; and the safety spring, the last two items not shown. The safety catch engaged a recess in the cocking piece, bottom, which was secured to the bolt and striker. When activated, the safety assembly prevented the striker from moving forward or the bolt from operating.

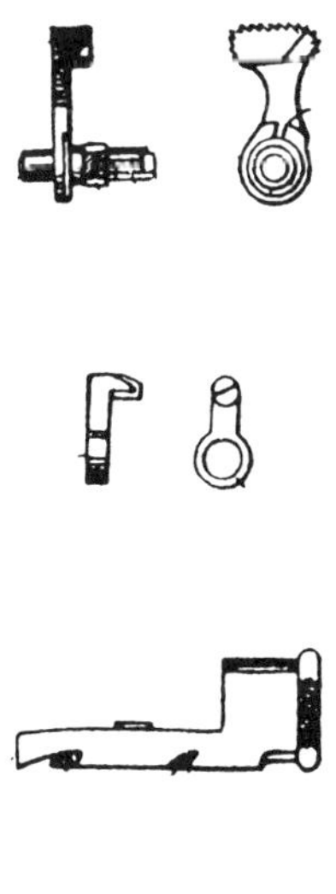

butt swivel was inletted into the butt stock, instead of being screwed in on a single pedestal mount.

Further, the keeper screw on the striker was redesigned with a slot large enough to be turned by a coin, in case it became necessary to dismount the bolt in the field. However, this was greatly frowned upon by the British armourers, most of whom believed that a trooper should never mess about with so complicated a mechanism as a rifle.

Otherwise, the Mark I* has the same front and rearsights, volley sights, handguards, charger guide, and nosecap as the Mark I.

Ultimately, these changes made the rifle slightly heavier than its predecessor, bringing the total weight to 8 pounds 7 ounces.

Many Number 1 Mark I* rifles were returned to the arsenal for one reason or another — conversion to a later mark, modification of sights, repair of broken parts or furniture, or barrel replacement. Note that this rifle, #G954, had a previous identity earlier in its life. It is not unusual to see a serial number on the receiver ring crossed out, and superceded by another stamped number.

The long range sights on the Mark I* were inlet into the left side of the forend, and affixed at the safety assembly, as shown here. When not in use, the rear long range pointer was folded forward where it rested along the top edge of the forend.

The rearsight on the Number 1 Mark I* was the same type as on the earlier Mark I model, featuring a sliding leaf with a "V" notch battle sight. The leaf had settings to 2,000 yards, along with the provision of a windgauge to set the sight for deflection.

The bolthead charger guide of the Mark I* rifle is shown in position with the bolt closed. Note the scalloped area in the left of the receiver where the thumb would strike when stripping a clip of rounds into the magazine.

Number 1 Mark I**

The Number 1 Mark I** was a Mark I rifle, upgraded to reflect the Mark III improvements.

Rifle, Short, Magazine, Lee Enfield, Mark I (Number 1 Mark I**)**

Approved on 4 January 1908, this rifle was a Mark I, upgraded to feature some of the improvements of the Mark III rifle. Converted for Royal Navy use, changes were made to the Mark I sighting — the "U" notch of the Mark III rearsight replaced the "V" notch, while the foresight was the new blade type.

Other minor modifications were made to the rifle, including fitting a slotted keeper screw to the cocking piece, a new charger guide, removing the magazine link loop, and adding a sling swivel at front of the trigger guard.

Number 1 Mark I***

World War I and the adoption of new ammunition led to the Number 1 Mark I*** rifle.

Rifle, Short, Magazine, Lee Enfield, Mark I* (Number 1 Mark I***)**

This variation of the Number 1 series was officially approved on 22 April 1914 and was brought about by the Army's adoption of the Mark VII .303 cartridge. Accordingly, the sights on Mark I* rifles needed alteration for the new service round, necessitating the new model, the Mark I***.

The changes were accomplished by fitting a new blade foresight to the rifle, while the rearsight underwent a complete replacement. The new rearsight was the same as that fitted to the Mark III, with a "U" notch, a wind gauge adjusted by a spring screw, and graduations from 200 to 2000 yards.

The rifle carries the charger bridge mounted on the bolthead, as its predecessors did. It also has a cutoff, the long range dial sights, and all the other features of the earlier marks.

The action of the Number 1 Mark I* rifle clearly shows the traits of its predecessors in the bolthead charger guide, magazine cutoff, and markings on the right side of the butt socket. The rifle shown was manufactured in 1905 by the Birmingham Small Arms Company.**

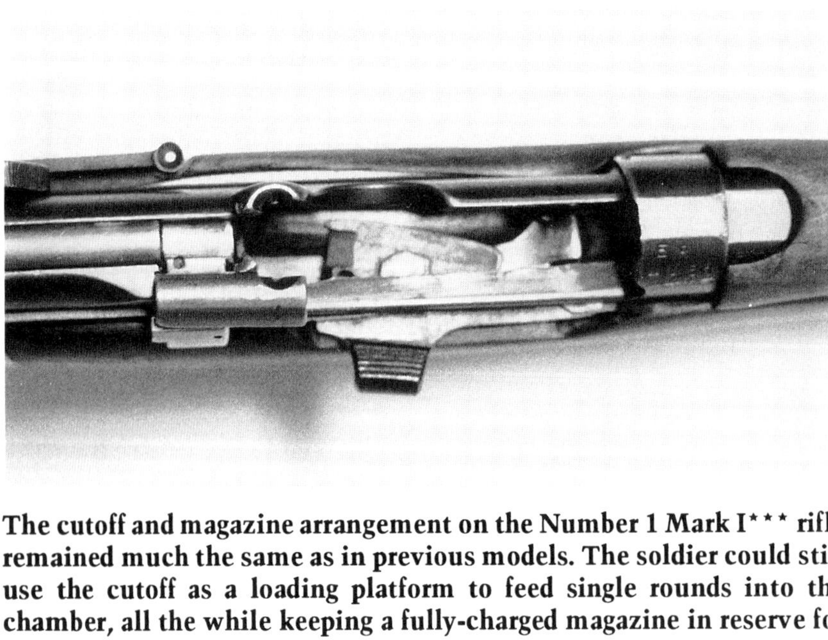

The cutoff and magazine arrangement on the Number 1 Mark I* rifle remained much the same as in previous models. The soldier could still use the cutoff as a loading platform to feed single rounds into the chamber, all the while keeping a fully-charged magazine in reserve for emergency use.**

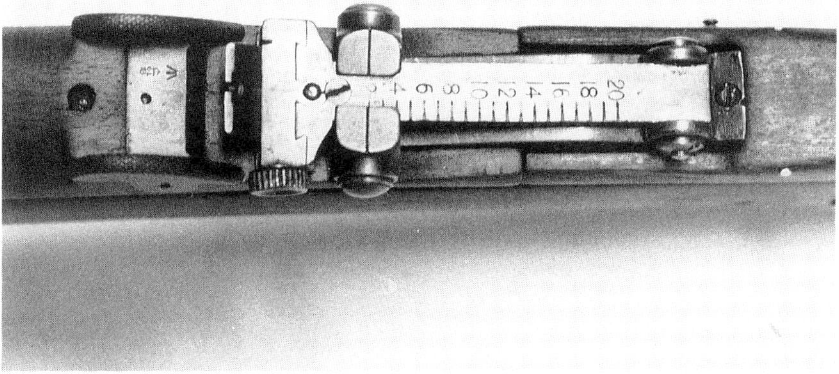

The rearsight on the Number 1 Mark I*** was usually altered due to the new service round then adopted. On this Mark I***, the earlier rearsight has been retained, but fitted with a "U" notch, instead of a "V." Note the broad arrow stamp and inspector's mark stamped into the handguard, in between the rearsight protection ears. The broad arrow was the indicator of acceptance into service.

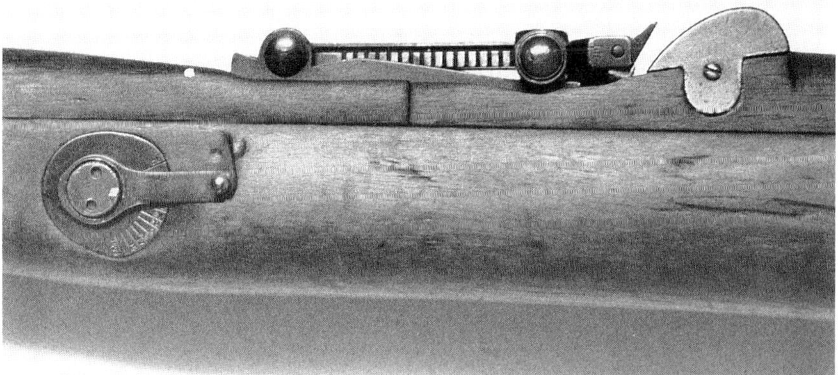

Long range dial sights, also called volley sights, continued to be used on the Number 1 Mark I*** rifle. The dial plate was inletted into the left side of the forend, and had an aiming pointer attached. The rear pointer of the dial sight was attached at the safety lever. Together, the two parts were used for volley fire at ranges greater than 1,500 yards.

A close look at the butt socket of this Mark I* rifle provides a wealth of information. From top to bottom are the royal cypher with Edward VII's initials; the manufacturer's identity, BSA Co., Sparkbrook; the year of manufacture, 1906; and the model designation, Short Lee Enfield Mark I***.**

Number 1 Mark I Cond.

Rifle, Short, Magazine, Lee Enfield, Converted Mark I (Number 1 Mark I Cond.)

Converted from Lee Metford Mark I and Mark I* rifles, this model was officially adopted as a conversion on 2 November 1903. The right side of the butt socket will identify the parentage of the rifle, retaining all the information of the original Lee Metford or Lee Enfield. The conversion marks were placed on the left side of the socket.

This conversion was never really manufactured, other than some sample patterns, although it exists as an official conversion.

It was modified to resemble the Number 1 Mark I externally by fitting a SMLE barrel, forend, front and rear handguards.

The Lee Metford bolt assembly was replaced with a Mark I bolt and bolthead, and a safety assembly was added to the left of the action body.

The modified rifle also sported the Mark I's new windage-adjustable rearsight, as well as the new barleycorn foresight and nosecap. The rearsight was graduated the same as the Mark I, to 2,000 yards, and the rifle included the long range dial plate and aperture rearsight.

Number 1 Mark II Cond.

Rifle, Short, Magazine, Lee Enfield, Converted Mark II (Number 1 Mark II Cond.)

Made from Lee Metford Mark II and II* rifles and Lee Enfield Mark I and I* rifles, this model was officially adopted as a conversion on 16 January 1903. As with previous conversions, the right side of the butt socket carries the identifying marks of the parentage of the rifle, retaining all the information of the original Lee Metford or Lee Enfield. The conversion marks were placed on the left side of the socket.

In order to modify the rifles to the new mark, the British added a new safety catch, and fitted the new SMLE magazine. Those rifles which had lugs on the bolt rib for a dustcover had the lugs removed.

Of course, the new SMLE barrels were fitted to the converted rifles, with new wood in the form of forends, and front and rear handguards replacing the Lee Metford and Long Lee Enfield furniture. Appropriate metal fittings were added as necessary.

Further, a charger guide was added to the boltheads of the rifles, to bring them up to the Mark I standard.

Number 1 Mark II* Cond.

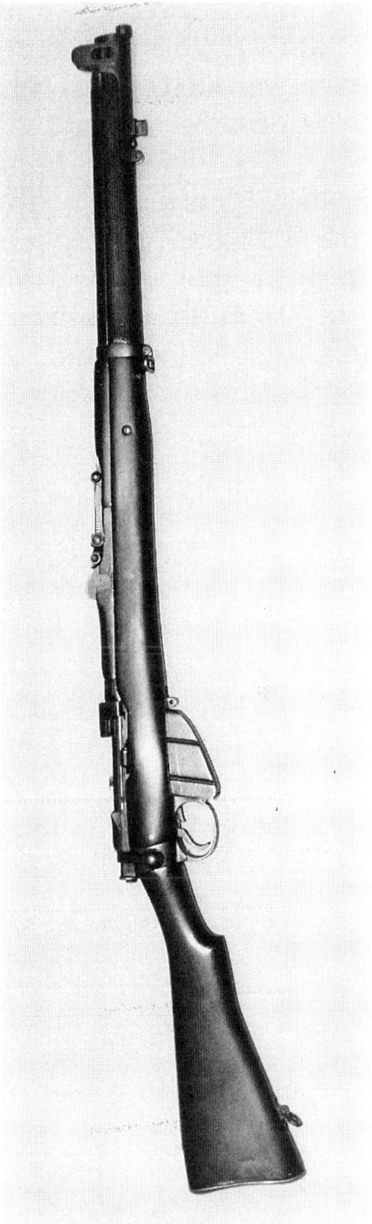

The Number 1 Mark II* Converted was approved 2 July 1906.

Rifle, Short, Magazine, Lee Enfield, Converted Mark II*
(Number 1 Mark II* Cond.)

Approval for this mark was granted on 2 July 1906. This model was a conversion of the same rifles as the Mark II Cond., and the chief difference lies in the fact that the Mark II* had a sheet steel buttplate, instead of one made of gunmetal.

The balance of the conversion was done the same as the Mark II Cond.

Number 1 Mark II** Cond.

Rifle, Short, Magazine, Lee Enfield, Converted Mark II**
(Number 1 Mark II Cond.)**

The British were nothing, if not thorough, and this model only bears evidence to that fact. This conversion, authorized for the Navy on 25 June 1908, took the Mark II Converted rifle and converted it to the Mark I** pattern.

Several years later, the Mark II** Cond. rifles were improved again, this time to fit them to Number 1 Mark III specifications.

Number 1 Mark I** IP

The Ishapore pattern conversion was done during the first decade of the 20th century.

Rifle, Short, Magazine, Lee Enfield, Mark I India Pattern (Number 1 Mark I** IP)**

It is usual to find this rifle converted to Number 1 Mark III specifications, from either British-made or Indian-manufactured rifles.

Conversions of Indian Mark I* IP and British SMLE Mark I rifles took place early in the twentieth century, with the conversion markings of the date and arsenal being stamped on the left of the socket.

The markings on this Number 1 Mark I IP are the royal cypher; the Ishapore arsenal name, where the rifle was manufactured; and the model designation.**

Number 1 Mark III

The Number 1 Mark III was the workhorse of the British Army during the First World War.

Rifle, Short, Magazine, Lee Enfield, Mark III (Number 1 Mark III)

The change to the Mark III rifle was approved on 26 January 1907, and differed from the Mark I and Mark I* rifles by having different front and rear sights, a new rear handguard, and an improved type of charger loading.

On the Number 1 Mark III, the barleycorn foresight installed on all previous models of service rifle was now gone, and in its place was a simple blade. The design of the blade featured straight sides, which could be supplied in five different heights, instead of the barleycorn's sloping sides.

The five sizes were 1.00 inch, 1.015 inch, 1.03 inch 1.045 inch, and 1.06 inch. The size of each blade referred only to its height above the axis of the bore, not to blade length or any other measure.

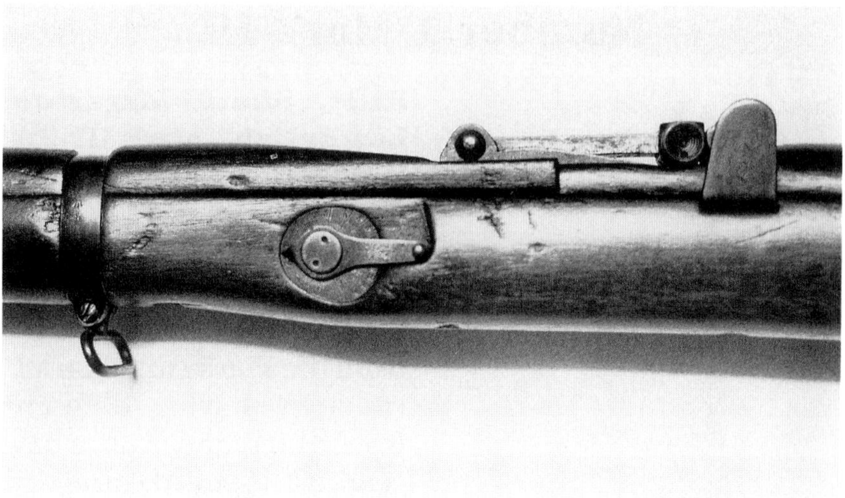

The long range sights on the Number 1 Mark III rifle served the same function as those on previous models, consisting of the dial plate and pointer inletted into the left side of the forearm, and a rear pointer attached at the safety lever at the left rear of the action.

The rearsight of the Number 1 Mark III was an area which saw one of the biggest changes from preceeding rifles. In addition to modifying and strengthening the rearsight bed and the manner in which it was attached to the barrel, the improved rearsight also featured a "U" notch instead of the "V" found on the rifle's predecessors.

In order to allow for finer adjustments, the rearsight featured a worm wheel arrangement on the right side of the slide. By pressing a catch on the left side of the rearsight leaf, the worm wheel was disengaged from notches on the right of the leaf, and the slide could be moved to the required setting. This method proved to be much quicker to manipulate than the previous type of slide and catch.

Graduations on the rearsight were from 200 to 2000 yards on the right side of the leaf, while graduations on the left side marked off intervals of 25 yards each. Since the worm wheel

The Mark III rifle featured a modern charger bridge securely attached to the receiver, instead of the previous type on the bolthead. Note the rear pointer of the long range sights in the firing position, and the inletted part of the stock, where it folds forward.

on the slide had ten notches in it, each notch represented 5 yards in range. In this way, very fine adjustments could be made to the Mark III's rearsight, which provided the infantryman with the opportunity to truly zero his rifle in changing conditions.

The windgauge found on previous models also underwent some changes by being simplified and improved, and the wheel used to make adjustments was made easier to handle. Each 90-degree turn on the windgauge wheel was one minute of angle at 100 yards.

In addition to the rearsight change, a modification also was made to the rearsight protector. Instead of having a pair of metal ears attached to the rear handguard, as in previous marks, the new rearsight protector was a larger and heavier model, inletted and screwed into the forend. The ears extended vertically from the forend and along the sides of the back of the rearsight, protecting it from any inad-

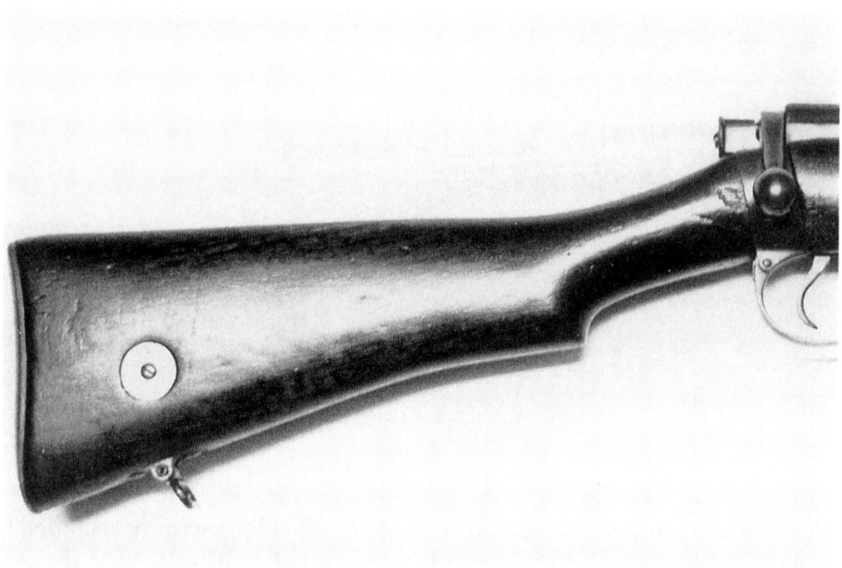

The butt stock of the Mark III rifle continued the use of a butt marking disc, which was generally stamped with regimental or other unit markings.

vertent damage which it might receive from the sides.

The volley sights were continued on the Number 1 Mark III rifle too, but with a minor change. On this model, the dial plate inletted into the left front side of the forend was now graduated from 1,600 to 2,800 yards.

Another major alteration to the Mark III rifle was the inclusion of a fixed charger bridge to the rifle's receiver, in place of the sliding charger guide on the bolthead of the Mark I rifle. The fixed bridge, in addition to being much more robust than the sliding charger guide, also served to stiffen the action somewhat.

It now became much easier for an infantryman to load his magazine through the new charger bridge, and if he left the charger in the bridge after stripping the cartridges into the rifle, it was no problem. The design of the charger bridge allowed the bolt to be closed on a charger and force it from the body without interfering with the operation of the rifle.

Since the charger bridge had been relocated to the rifle's receiver, the bolthead now took on a different shape. It no longer required the stud to which was affixed the sliding charger guide, which helped simplify manufacture of the bolthead itself.

The bolt body, cocking piece, striker, striker spring, extractor, extractor spring and assorted screws on the bolt all took much the same character on the Number 1 Mark III rifle as they did on the previous Number 1 models.

And in addition, the trigger and trigger guard assembly also mirrored their earlier counterparts. The trigger was still pinned to the trigger guard, and retained the two nubs which bore on the lower arm of the sear. This produced the two-stage pull know on military rifles.

Accordingly, the internal

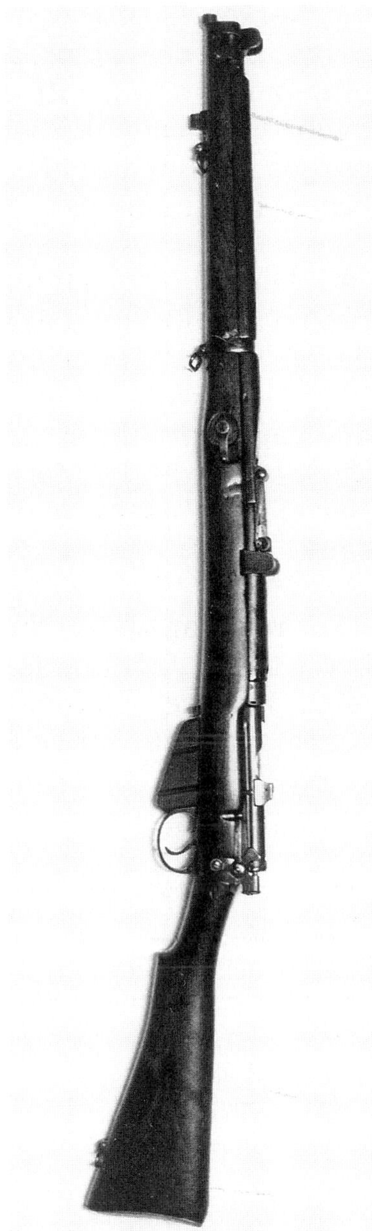

A full length view of the Number 1 Mark III rifle shows the long range dial sights, along with the redesigned rearsight and its protection ears.

receiver parts of the sear, sear spring, cross pins, and magazine catch all remained basically the same as those in the earlier Number 1 Mark I models.

Enfield rifling of left hand twist was continued in the barrels installed on Mark III models, with the groove and land depth the same as those on the SMLE Mark 1. Barrel length also was the same.

The nosecap on the Number 1 Mark III rifle was altered, however, so that the ears lost their inward curve and changed their shape to a more angular pattern. This helped to allow more light to reach the foresight, which it was hoped, would improve shooting at moving targets. The nosecap also was lightened to make the rifle less muzzle heavy.

Some minor modifications were made to the front handguard in regard to its thickness, and the rifle's forend was modified to accept the new rearsight protector.

The butt stock was continued in three lengths —

Mark III Bolthead

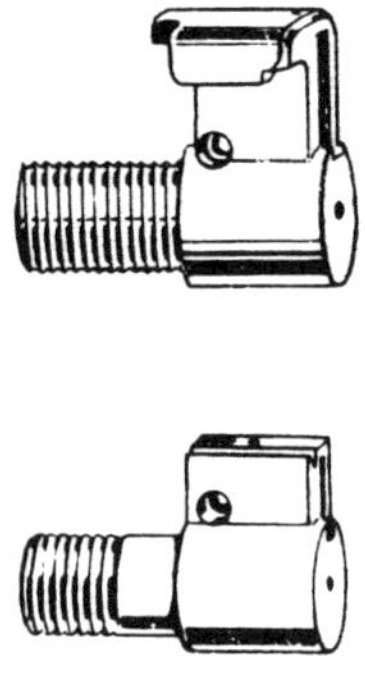

The bolthead of the Number 1 Mark III rifle, top left, was quite different in profile to that of the later Number 4 Mark 1 rifle, bottom left. The Mark III bolthead closely followed the pattern of its earlier bretheren. In addition, the Number 1 Mark III boltheads were not marked with sizes, as were those manufactured for the Number 4 rifle.

The Mark III Rearsight

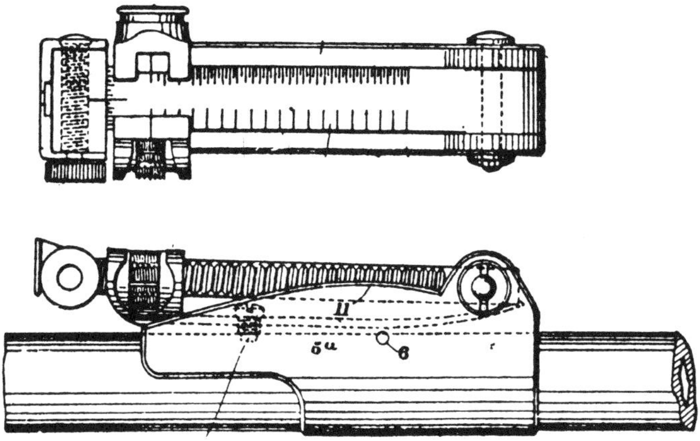

The rearsight of the Number 1 Mark III rifle was simplified and improved, chiefly in the overall design.

normal, short and long — with a trapped butt plate, butt swivel and butt marking disc.

Overall weight of the Number 1 Mark III, without bayonet, was 8 pounds 10-1/2 ounces.

Mark VII Ammunition

It is ironic that the adoption of Mark VII ammunition as standard for the British Service, on 3 November 1910, was considered a temporary expedient rather than a permanent solution. At the time, it was seen as a stop-gap measure until the introduction of an entirely new design of rifle and ammunition. In the end, Mark VII ammunition served through two World Wars, the Korean war, and numerous colonial conflicts. The round is still loaded commercially today.

The major difference between the Mark VII round and that of its predecessor, the Mark VI, was the bullet, which was dramatically different in shape in weight. The Mark VII was pointed and weighed 174 grains, in contrast to the earlier round nose 215 grain Mark VI. The new bullet had a core of lead-antimony, and was surrounded in a cupro-nickel jacket.

The charge of the new round was 37 grains of modified tubular cordite, while the case was of solid drawn brass. The cartridge was Berdan primed, and weighed about 386 grains.

When loaded with nitro-cellulose powder, the round was designated the mark VIII Z. These cartridges were used chiefly in machine guns.

Better accuracy at longer ranges and greater penetration were two of the chief attributes of the Mark VII ammunition.

Number 1 Mark III*

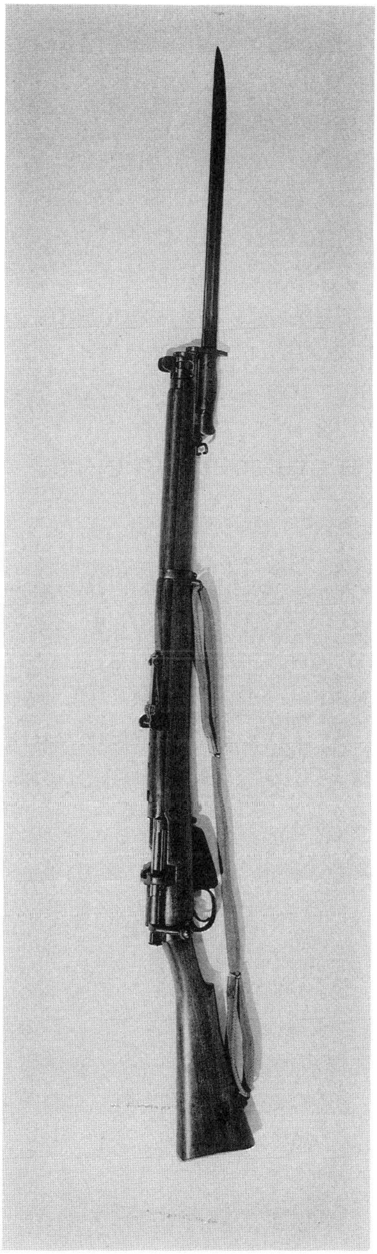

The Number 1 Mark III* was a simplified version of the Mark III.

Rifle, Short, Magazine, Lee Enfield, Mark III* (Number 1 Mark III*)

This rifle was a wartime model, officially adopted on 2 January 1916. Since so many Englishmen were now involved in the First World War as soldiers, the need for more and more rifles grew daily. One of the ways in which the British government decided it could speed up deliveries of rifles to the troops was by simplification of the rifles themselves. Thus, the Mark III* (pronounced "mark three, star") was born.

Several modifications were carried out on the Mark III* which distinguished it from it's earlier brother.

The magazine cutoff was omitted from the Mark III*. This saved a considerable amount of machine time, since deleting the cutoff meant that the receiver no longer needed to be drilled and slotted. Also, the necessity for a screw to fix the cutoff to the receiver was gone.

The long range dial sights also were omitted from the modified rifle. This meant that the forearm no longer had to be drilled to accept the front dial sight plate and cross screw. In addition, there was a considerable savings in time and material in not fitting the front dial plate and the rear aperture for the dial sights.

Another change was the omission of the rearsight windgauge. Manufacture of this mechanism to provide deflection in the rearsight was deemed too costly for its value, and it was deleted from the Mark III*. The windgauge was replaced with a fixed end with a rough blackened textured finish, fitted with a U notch.

In addition, the trigger guard's swivel loops were omitted, and replaced by a wire loop. The wire loop was easier to fabricate than the swivel loops, which had been drilled and tapped.

Further, the contour of the cocking piece was changed from a knurled knob to a slab-sided piece with finger grooves. The Mark III* also omitted the piling swivel lug and the butt marking disc.

Number 1 Mark V

Rifle, Short, Magazine, Lee Enfield, Mark V (Number 1 Mark V)

This weapon was made in limited numbers from 1922 to 1924, when the British services were experimenting with a longer sight radius on the service rifle in order to improve accuracy.

The Mark V was the first of the Lee Enfield series to sport a tangent peepsight at the rear of the receiver. By providing a longer base for sighting, the theorists maintained, improvements in accuracy could be made. In this case, the sighting base on the Mark V was slightly over 30 inches in length.

The rearsight was a folding aperture type, with graduations from 200 to 1,400 yards. It was possible to position the sight not only at at 90 degrees to the axis of the bore, but also at an angle of 45 degrees. It had a release latch to the left side of the sight in

The Number 1 Mark V was the first Lee Enfield with a rearsight on the action, rather than the barrel.

order to operate the slide.

Since the rearsight was not affixed to the rear of the receiver, it was not necessary to have any other type of rearsight or base assembly on the barrel.

This meant a few changes in the handguard and forend assemblies. The rear handguard was lengthened to just over 12 inches long in order to cover the area previously taken up by the rearsight assembly. Essentially, it extended forward from the receiver ring to the lower band. It continued to be held in position on the barrel by use of a double spring assembly at the rear, but was secured at the front by the lower band.

The front handguard was not much changed, except it too was kept in place by bands — the lower band at the rear, and a new upper band at the front.

This new upper band held a piling swivel, and was set into recessed cut into the front handguard and the forend.

The right socket of the Number 1 Mark V is marked with the royal cypher, the place of manufacture, the date, and the model.

Two views of the Number 1 Mark V rearsight, which was the first of its kind on any Lee Enfield series rifle. Prior to this, Lee Enfield rearsights were affixed to the barrel. By moving the rearsight to the action of the weapon, the sight radius was lengthened, thus increasing the potential accuracy of the firearm. The peepsight aperture also was a departure from previous British rearsights, which had been either open "V" or "U" notches until the Mark V was introduced.

The nosecap of the Mark V rifle was similar to that on the Mark III, with the exception of an additional band at its rear. A stacking swivel was secured to the band.

The forend was very similar to that on the Mark III rifle, except that it no longer had recesses cut for the long range dial sights, the rearsight protector and rearsight.

The Mark V had a provision for a cutoff, as did the Mark III rifle.

Further changes in the Mark V rifle included omitting the long range dial sights, as was done on the Mark III* rifles, since this saved the extra manufacture time on the rifle and on the sights, as well as the material of the dial plate and apertures themselves.

While many Number 1 Mark V rifles were manufactured and put through trials, the rifle was not officially introduced into service. It ultimately became obsolete, and was superseded by the next mark of rifle.

Number 1 Mark VI

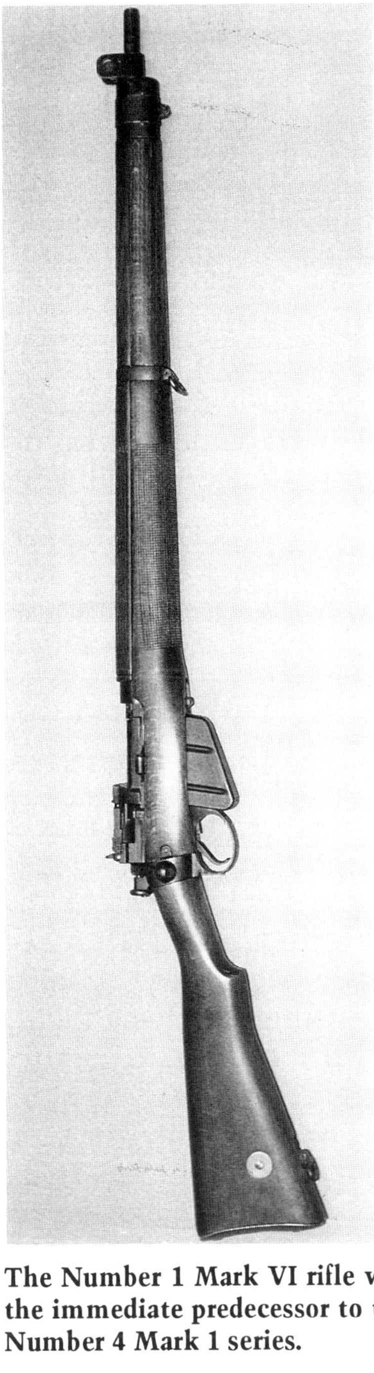

The Number 1 Mark VI rifle was the immediate predecessor to the Number 4 Mark 1 series.

Rifle, Short, Magazine, Lee Enfield, Mark VI (Number 1 Mark VI)

The next step in the succession of the Lee Enfield Number 1 series of rifles was the development of the Number 1 Mark VI. This rifle, first built in 1926, was a completely new design which featured a departure from the full-stocked earlier marks.

While three different patterns were produced, the Mark VI rifle actually never went into full production. Approximately 3,600 rifles were made up as troop trials rifles, but production never proceeded much past that stage.

The Mark VI was a further simplified version of the Mark V model. One of the more noticable features of the Mark VI was the new receiver, cut with relatively flat sides, and highlighted by lightening cuts and recesses. The side of the receiver was lower than other rifles in the Number 1 series, slightly more square in contour, and had a deep scoop cut out of it on the left rear side.

The charger guide and rearsight base on the new receiver were also redesigned from previous models.

The barrel of the new rifle was much stiffer than that on earlier Number 1 marks, thus showing an improvement in accuracy. It was 25 inches long, and carried lugs at the muzzle for affixing a bayonet and the front sight block. With the heavier barrel, the British thought that such a rifle also would serve well as a sniper rifle.

Another noticable feature of the Mark VI was the redesigned forend, which allowed a portion of the muzzle to protrude. This was a radical change from the earlier marks where the forend went to the muzzle, capped by the heavy nosecap. The forend also was notable since it had deep-cut chequering of a rather coarse, square pattern.

Further, the rifle carried a cutoff, as did many of its predecessors.

Since the rearsight of the weapon was on the receiver, the handguards were redesigned to be of nominally equal length. The front handguard was secured to the barrel and forend by front and lower bands, while the rear handguard was secured by the lower band and a handguard ring.

The rearsight was another major departure from that on the traditional British service rifle. It was a double aperture sight, graduated to 1,300 yards, which folded into a small recess in the top of the receiver. The fixed battle sight was usable when the sight was folded down, and an aperture finely adjusted for elevation was available when the sight was flipped up for use. There was no adjustment for deflection.

The foresight block on the

rifle was completely redesigned, and set on special lugs milled onto the rifle's barrel. The foresight block had a key inset into its front, which secured the foresight blade.

The Mark VI rifle bolt also was redesigned to fit the new receiver. The bolthead was made much smaller and more compact than those on other Number 1 series rifles, and the bolt body was of a slightly different form. In addition, the cocking piece, striker and striker screw also had been changed to reflect the more streamlined receiver.

Bayonets for the Number 1 Rifle

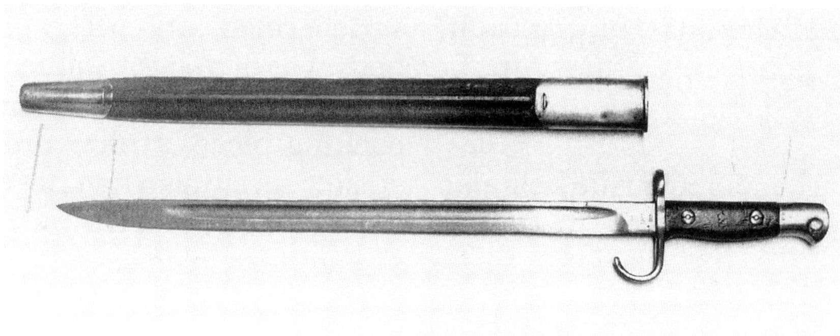

Bayonets for the Number 1 series rifles included the hooked quillion bayonet, top, and the Pattern 1907, bottom, both shown with their respective scabbards.

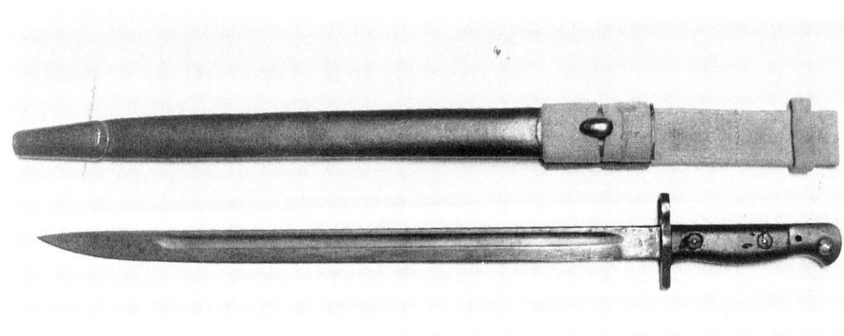

Acknowledgements

It is most gratifying to have friends and acquaintances who are willing to make firearms in their collections available to be photographed.

The author is indebted to Bob Maze for his excellent photographs of several firearms in his collection, as well as to Bob Washburn, Dennis Lewis, and Mike Cipressy for their loan of various Number 1 rifles.

Bibliography

Other publications on Lee Enfield rifles:

The British Service Lee, by Ian Skennerton. Published by Arms & Armour Press, London.

The Lee Enfield Number 4 Rifles, by Alan M. Petrillo. Published by Excalibur Publications, Latham, NY.

The Lee Enfield Rifle, by Major E.G.B. Reynolds. Published by Herbert Jenkins, London.

Small Arms of the World, Revised, by W.H.B. Smith. Published by the Stackpole Co., Harrisburg, Pa.

Modern Small Arms, by Major Frederick Myatt MC. Published by Crescent Books, New York.

About the Author

Alan M. Petrillo is an enthusiast of British firearms and military history, and is the owner of British Arms Company Ltd.

He is the author of **The Lee Enfield Numer 4 Rifles,** and has had articles published in ***Military History*** and other publications.